# The Slow Turning of Wonderful Things

## Beatrice Drake

BookLeaf
Publishing

India | USA | UK

Presentation by *BookLeaf Publishing*

Web: www.bookleafpub.com

E-mail: info@bookleafpub.com

ISBN: 9789357445047

First edition 2022

To Mama,

everything good in me came from you.

# ACKNOWLEDGEMENT

The author would like to acknowledge Antoinette Tapia and John Clark for their decades of exceptional professional feedback, creativity, and encouragement.

The author would also like to thank Obert Skye for his constant support; they say never meet your idols, but Obert is the exception to that rule.

The author would like to extend her gratitude to Josef Hefkin, Haley Hofmann, Ben Spotts, Braelin Love and all the members of the Fun Unorthodox Kids for their company and enthusiasm during this project, and basically every other day, too.

The author would finally like to thank her friends and family across the globe for their continued kindness and support.

# PREFACE

A door left open
just a tiny little bit,
letting the sun in.

# Orange Blossoms

Know that, one day, my love,
we will lounge in the sun
under our orange trees in bloom,
as the distant thunder roars around us
in the garden we have built.
It is wondrous, effortless, though we have to
tame the weeds
and prune the bushes,
it is perfect work.

After all this time,
our love will taste like fresh orange blossoms
and sound like the symphony when songbirds
meet in the swaying branches with joyous
delight,
and will feel warm like the July sunshine
between sweeping curtains of rain.
We were always worthy of this.

But now, as the long winter ends and pulls
back its ice from the ground,
I am shaking off the haunted nightmares
that gripped my sullen heart
and staked me to barren land,
and using the trickles of melted snow
to find my way to rich dirt.

I am learning to plant the gardens
under whose canopies we will one day raise our
children.

And know, my darling, though we cannot
understand it yet,
your love is deep and worthy and lasting,
because it is a force to match mine,
for as much as I love dancing to my own beat,
I want to hear your steady rhythm click against
the old floorboards.
For as much as I love the warmth of the evening
passing
in my own company,
I know our silence is more comfortable together.
For as much as I love the taste of an orange,
it is all the sweeter to share.

So I will keep going, for now, roaming the wide
earth,
to find fertile land for the start of a garden
where our oranges can grow wild in the sun.

# Lily Henriette

She's a junkyard dog and
if you look at her right in the harsh noon sun,
maybe she looks a little like a weather-beaten
outlaw
just trying to buy a shot of whiskey at the
saloon.

She got scars,
more than any dog I've seen
and she's missing a leg,
The front one, where long, precise cuts have
stitched her back together;
So honestly, maybe she looks a little like
Frankenstein's dog.

She sighs loudly,
a forlorn sound,
like she's lived her whole life
fighting off some preventable disease
on a homestead in the middle of a corn field on
the American Plains.

And because she's missing a shoulder,
she can wiggle out of almost any harness,
like a travelling magician who's almost got the
trick down.

We joke, albeit on the square,
that if she had all her legs, she'd be too fast to
catch,
like a silver racecar from the 20's.
And it's funny until you remember
that she was hit by a car.

When I met her, I was told she was nervous
around humans,
to not make eye contact. To wait until she was
ready.
But she hobbled straight over to me,
and jumped up with one great claw,
with her blue eyes and radar dish ears,
and licked my face.

I didn't pick her,
she found me.
She's full of sad stories that I can't ever hear,
but I try to listen anyway.

I'd like to think that, in another world,
she's a pirate dog, with a peg leg and an eye
patch,
and she's crossed the Indian Ocean with the
Gunsway Haul
to settle into a life of anonymity
on my couch.

# September

It is the first of September, the rain stays low to
the ground,
and I have been happy for nine months.
Not all the time, mind you,
but the Big Sad hasn't oozed its way under my
door
in countless nights.

In fact, the longer that I live,
the smaller the Big Sad feels.

It's the end of summer,
and the wind shakes loose the dead needles from
the tree in the backyard,
and I find space in my chest to breathe.
And the sad thoughts no longer steal the
steadiness in my knees,
or the strength of my voice.
And the Big Sad sits in the nosebleed seats.
I move on.

The Big Sad isn't Big forever,
Though in those early days, it felt like it was and
would be,
always.

Fall approaches, warm and familiar,
And I have been happy for almost a year.
Not every moment of every day,
But the Big Sad has left its Goliath costume at
home,
And David's been able to put down his sword
Long enough for me to pit pounds of sweet
summer cherries for a pie.

It's hard, I'm not saying it wasn't hard.
But it was worth it
to be here,
in September.

# hispanohablantes

If I have learned anything it's,
'Don't judge someone by their English.'
We spend far too much time fixated of fissures
of grammatical fact,
and not actually hearing what someone else is
saying.

You don't have to write like I do
and your words don't have to sound like mine,
and in fact, your intelligence isn't quantifiable
by your capitalization.

Don't mistake angry correction for intelligent
contradiction,
and anytime you make a 'mistake' in front of
me,
know that I do not care.

A Mexican woman stands on a stage,
she pauses the concert long enough to speak into
the microphone,
and she says, 'I'm sorry, my English is not very
pretty.'
I think about that a lot.

I speak Spanish with an accent, because of
course I do.
and often I start with, 'Lo siento, mi Español no
es muy bonita.'
so I hear you
I hear you a thousand times.
My English is a product of years of privilege,
and location, and circumstance,
and I've answered enough calls from my family
in Juarez
to know that English isn't cut and dry.
it isn't logical, or easy.
and if I had to use my Spanish against
cruel people with a penchant for perfection,
I'd never speak at all.

Entonces,
lo siento, mi Español no es muy bonita,
Pero, creo que debes tener orgullosa.

# The Garden Sidewalk

Life does not stop for grief.
The rain slips slowly from silver clouds
and disappears into the hot concrete,
and I hold grief close.
It seems, of all the perches I could find
to let my rage and sorrow bubble,
the sidewalk in my mother's garden
is the perfect spot.
A hummingbird flits by, trilling into the electric
air
and it feels like I should be dying,
but the rain rolls over,
and the feeling seeps out into the ground,
until I am just dirt.
And in the pouring rain,
I, again, can breathe.
Life does not stop for grief,
because that is not the purpose of grief.

# Wellspring I

13

The Wellspring of Hope
ponders its place in the world
as hatred abounds.

# Wellspring II

The Wellspring runs dry
as the last human forgets
the way kindness feels.

# Wellspring III

15

We soon realize
the only way hope can live
is to dig deeper.

# Love Shaped like Pink-and-Golden Hearts

They're the newlyweds of a Hallmark movie,
Bound together in a holy Vegas wedding.
They have names like Bright and Pure.
It's cotton candy sweet,
the way they fit together.

I wonder if love can still be so luminescent
in the wake of so much haggard effort,
if love will ever feel so young again.
He carries her across the threshold of their new
home,
where they will live their lovely lives.

I am not a fool, I know
this love will weather many storms,
but I'm not callous enough to expect their boat to
break.
If anyone is rooting for love
with reckless surety,
let it always be me.

## humans

I don't know what makes us human
I don't know what makes all of it.
But I know what makes part of it.

It's the way we drop into smoke and battle
flames to save each other,
the way we dedicate years of our lives to learn
how to perform chest compressions
and sew our wounds back together.

It's the way we sign our names in the letters we
send
to our favorite people in the world,
and the tenderness of the way we bring flowers
to the graves of our grandparents.

It's the gentleness of holding hands
along a bridge decorated with padlocks
engraved with initials of long-lost lovers.

We sent a record into space
with pictures of our planet,
and songs from The Golden Flute,
so civilizations can know about us.
The best of us.

We don't do it perfectly,
it being all.

I don't know what makes us human
and I don't know what makes all of it.
But I know what makes part of it.

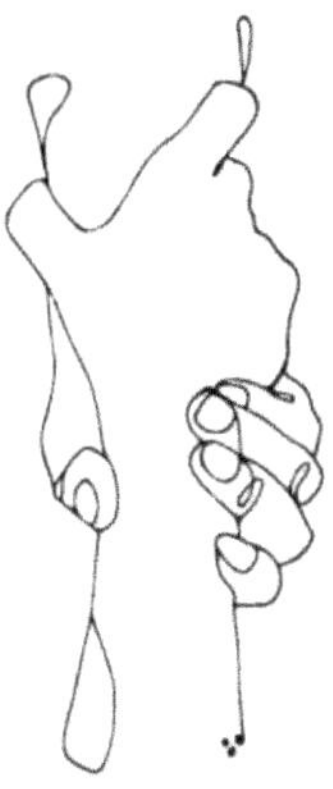

# Star Crawler

Someday she will see the earth from the sky,
and her feet will walk on stardust.
She will have a silver spaceship,
with a decal airbrushed on the side,
and a one-way ticket to the cosmos.
She will show you her helmet, and how it fits
over the
head of brown hair you brushed everyday
when she was a little girl.

She will be a Star Crawler,
she was born for this.

But it will take her down paths that she never
expected:
she will choke on the dust
of a thousand burning planets,
and she will struggle to see through
the darkness of a black hole,
Her ship will be battered and beaten by a
thousand asteroids,
and she will lose herself in the space between
stars.

You won't be able to help her, though you want
to,

because she must walk this path alone,
billions of miles away.
Remember then that Star Crawlers are forged in
the heart of suns
that have been alive for billions of years.

What we can do now,
is show her the sky,
marvel at its incomprehensible vastness.
Let's show her the beauty of new horizons,
and the value of perseverance.
We can show her that no matter how dark or
bleak or hopeless,
that her mind is her best tool,
her spirit is indomitable,
and challenge is an opportunity
to move, shift, pivot, and dance.
Let's teach her to be a sojourner,
moving through space with enough curiosity to
pick her up
and push her forward.
We can teach her wonder,
to seek it, to love it, to challenge it.
And, honestly,
though it will not make the hard things easier,
let her overwhelming belief in herself
always motivate her.

In all those years, when she

skips stones along lakes of some distant planet,
let her remember her place in the universe
is wherever her humanity can bloom.
Let her remember what you taught her.

She's a Star Crawler,
she was born for this.

# A Shout into the Universe

It's been a long time since we've talked, but I
just wanted to reach out
and see how you're doing
Yeah, it's kinda nuts,
but you probably know that.

Everything's been going alright,
though the world feels like it's shaking itself
apart
and I'm just used to the vibrations.
But sometimes, when I stop long enough,
I feel like I've got vertigo and
I can feel myself shaking apart, too.

But I just wanted to send you a note,
see if maybe there's something I'm missing,
because I feel like this is the start to something
big, scary, unstoppable.

But anyway, I guess, if I've got your attention for
a minute,
is there a way I could ask you a question?
Has it always felt like the world is ending?
Or is this... new?

Anyway, thank you so much for stopping to hear
me out.
I guess the only thing to do is keep going.
In spite, because, for, the best of us.
We have to keep going.

I hope you're doing okay, too.
I don't know what it looks like,
from all the way out there.
Do you get trapped in the sorrow?
Or do you just look for the beauty?

# The Ring

A fighter stands at the edge of the ring.
She's three rounds in,
and her lip is bleeding,
and her head hurts from a left-handed hook
she hadn't seen.

Her opponent has the reach
the weight
and the experience,
and calling her the underdog is more
an understatement than a courtesy.

The ref starts the round, and she's focused
defending
dodging
keeping her gloves to her cheeks.
At this point, the commentators are guessing
she's trying to lose with grace.
She's panting.
huffing,
gasping,
but there's no slowing her errant heartbeat.

Blood rushes to her head, and she wants to quit.
For a second, as another punch lands,
she wants to crumple onto the mat.

The floor looks comfortable, sweaty and
slippery,
and she'd like to close her eyes.

"Get out of this," her coach says
and she can't even tell if it's actually him,
or the memory of a thousand times he's chanted
"Get out of this."

She doesn't think she can, but she opens her
eyes,
razer sharp focus
dodging one punch and then another.

Getting out of this starts slowly.
She breathes.
Dodges.
Pivots.
Ducks.
Backs up,
breathes,
lunges.
Her opponent now has to work to get within
striking distance.

She sees a flash across the fighter's face, of
doubt, of
shaken resolve,
and she pounces.

It might not be enough, but it's the
foothold,
the jab,
and cross,
and she's landing punches,
staying light on her feet,
moving faster,
her tired arms no longer feel heavy.

"Get out of this," she says, mostly to herself,
striking true,
a glancing shot to the brow,
and the warrior across from her goes down.

# Gentle Wish Generator

May your tea stay warm, even when you forget
it,
and your water stay cold, even though it's been
in the car.

May you win the jackpot on a scratcher, or at
least always get your money back,
and may you find a couple stray dollars in your
wallet for cotton candy at a travelling circus.

May your shoes be shiny, or at least not scuffed
when you walk,
and your laces stay dry, though you've stepped in
a puddle.

May you never get another papercut, and no
splinters, either,
and if you break a bone, I hope you can paint
some flowers on the cast.

May your friends love your jokes, and may you
never sit through silence in the company of
people who do not know your worth.
And may you always, always know you're loved.

May your pillow forts defy physics, and your
wifi work in every corner of the apartment,
and your friends be available for important
phone calls on short notice.

I wish you all the green lights on the nights
when you're tired,
and all the red lights on the night when you've
got nowhere to be.

And may you always land on the right spot in a
cake walk, and always get the numbers in bingo,
and while we're at it, let's add a penchant for
obscure knowledge that always comes in handy
in conversation.

May you have a superpower, but always mistake
it for coincidence,
like never having spinach stuck in your teeth,
or always grabbing the exact number of hangers
you need to hang your laundry.

Sometimes our luck feels like it's stuck to the
boot heel of misfortune,
so for just a little while,
may your luck be kind,
and your gentile wishes be answered.

# The Way Your Laugh Sounds

It's a gremlin sound,
and loud.
Dear lord, it has never been quiet.
It hooks in the way your mother laughs,
but ramps up like your father.
If I had to describe it,
goblin-esque, crawling through a marsh on
hands and knees,
a pocket full of pilfered purses.
It sounds like that.
There's a squeak to it,
when you're laughing too much, a wheeze,
it goes quiet, and it looks like you're howling at
the moon.
Diaphragm shaking and, after a minute,
You're wiping tears from your eyes.
I love it.
Don't let anyone tell you that
the way your laugh shakes your bones
is too much.
It's not.
I would rather my life have a soundtrack of
a thousand wild and unbridled cackles
than polite giggles stifled behind gloved hands.
So lend me your laughter,
and let's color this life with it.

# The End

Something has to start
when something else ends,
but new beginnings are an art
and the lifespan of those choices depend
on putting the horse before the cart.

Don't get stuck in in the past,
or fear that you'll choose wrong
fate doesn't depend on one die that is cast
or the final note of some ringing swan song.
You need to know that life ever-changes, and it
moves fast.

Even a wrong choice can be right,
and the right choice can change with time.
Know that apathy is the only thing to fight,
and thinking you're stuck forever is a crime.
Keep your goal ahead of you, always in sight.

And in the future, when your children have
asked
what lessons they can comprehend
Remind them the job with which you were
tasked:
That angrily broken fences you have to mend

And cruel words spoken in malice unmasked.

Do not feel like I'm treating this with disregard;
I know more than most that it's not always easy,
and that leaving something old can leave you
marred.
But your strength is born from what you feel is
uneasy,
And you're ready for what makes life hard.

# A Love Letter to All My Best Friends

When I was in kindergarten,
I was invited to your birthday party.
Yours was my first friend's birthday,
and your dad entertained us by crushing soda
cans
in a contraption screwed to the wall,
and I will always think of you when I crush a
can for recycling.

When I was in fifth grade,
we buried a baseball under the swings in the
playground;
you were the first person I ever talked to for
hours
on a corded phone.
I'll always remember you when someone says,
"Thick as thieves,"
because it's how my mom described us, to which
I responded,
"Mom, we'd never steal."

When I became friends with you in middle
school,
you introduced me to new music.
Whenever I smell cornstarch on freshly
laundered clothes,

when I remember the horrors of middle school,
I think of you.

When I met you high school,
I didn't realize how much of me
you would make up.
I remember the nights we spent
piled on the sofa watching dumb movies.
Sneaking twenty people into the Hunger Games
on ten tickets.
Holding each other through breakups,
holding each other at prom.
I remember the good times,
and when I think of my biggest mistake,
It's letting you all go.

In college,
I met you by complete accident,
and three months later,
you asked me to be in your wedding.
I think of you almost every day
and I thank the universe for you
that you are so wonderful,
that I am so lucky,
that I could love someone so much.

When I think of you,
I think of us at Village Inn, eating breakfast at
9:00 PM,

orbiting each other
in separate crises,
and how much I needed to see your face.
I think of how much you've changed my life
since.
When I think of the friends you go to
in your worst hour,
I think of you.

You're not all in my life anymore
and that's okay.
Maybe I haven't even met you all yet.
But each of you made my life better.
I'm sorry for the mistakes that I've made,
and I'm trying my best to forget the worst,
and only remember the moments that made us
friends.
I hope you remember me the same way.

# Loving an Invisible North

The morning blooms slowly,
elastic sunlight seeping through the leaves of the
plants on the sill.
I stretch my hands in all four directions,
knowing that, at least once,
I am pointing to you.

The day rises from intimate darkness,
and I brew my coffee in the rays of shining light.
I can feel your breath on the wind,
the surefire sound of your heart,
and it's the beat I run to.

The mailbox is empty,
but I'm still putting letters in the outbox.
I know, one day, your handwriting
will be as familiar to me as the lines around
your eyes when we are old,
after having spent decades laughing.

When I was young,
I'd stop and think about where you were, what
you were doing.
And, admittedly, I think about that a lot, now.
Maybe you're buying soup and cold medicine,
or adopting a dog from the shelter.

Maybe it's your mom's birthday,
or maybe you've got a flat tire on a highway
heading east.

The only thing that separates us now
is time.
I stretch my fingers in all four directions,
knowing, one day, you will be my north.

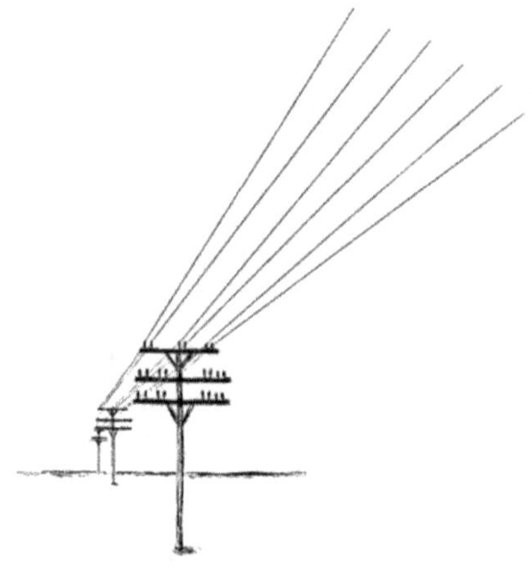

# Southwestern-Borne

Cut open my chest
and you'll see
that my heart bleeds the red dirt
seeping out of the arroyos during monsoon.
My bones are made of the granite bluffs,
straight and jagged and strong.
My tongue is made from the prickly pear,
round and spiked
powerful.
My breath is made from the
summer mists that settle between the mountain
valleys.
It's soft and striking.
My fingers are made from the curling grama
grass,
and my veins are made of bindweed.
My skin is the silt of the riverbed
that glows golden in the morning sun.
My hair is made of the night sky,
the inky, silk blackness.
I am made of my home,
and my home is home to many.
Everything good in myself
(the branches of my tree)
came from here
(will always be rooted in this place)

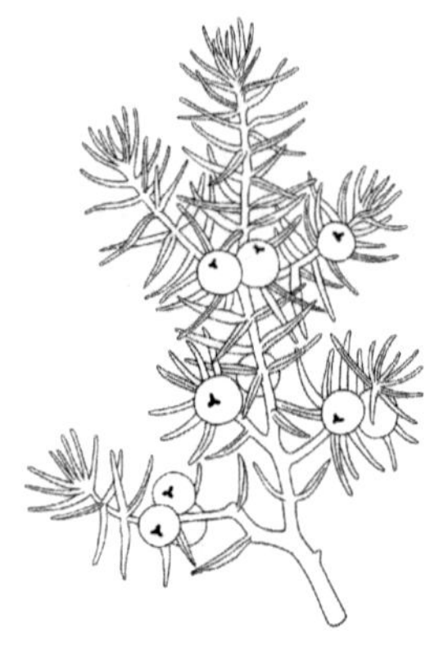

# The Storm and His Wrath

Help her
when you see her struggle.
That is my prayer for you.

The only way to stop the leak
is to stop the leak,
and while it seems obvious, it's hard to find
when the house is flooded.

Maybe it won't be apparent, like bricks breaking
apart the drywall,
maybe it will be invisible, like her biting her
tongue when she looks at you.
But when you notice it, trust that you're not
imagining it.

The oak tree is crooked from years of gale
winds,
but the gardener is here,
building supports out of plywood and straps.

All it takes sometimes,
is being there when no one else will be,
and listening when the days are hardest.

The cast is cumbersome,

and makes doing your hair impossible,
but you know your bones are knitting back
together.

You don't know it yet,
because I haven't told you,
but I was saved by the laughter of someone just
sitting beside me.

The morning dawns,
and the sickness is purged from the house,
and the windows are open for fresh air and
birdsong.

# Epilogue: Banishing the Beast from Under the Bed

I give you nothing good from my heart.
In fact, I have given back all of the things I took
from you.

I wonder what you kept of me,
I don't know what was left for you in the end.

I have kept nothing from you, and I give
everything you gave me back.
I give everything back.

I wonder what you keep of me,
I hope it is nothing.